The Book of the Giants: The Manichean and The Dead Sea Scroll apocryphal versions

W. B. Henning

Fabio R. Araujo

LAS VEGAS. IAP PUBLISHING © 2015

Table of Contents

Preface to this Edition   5

The Manichean Version   7

The Dead Sea Scroll Version   61

Preface to this Edition

The Book of Giants is an apocryphal book. Its discovery at Qumran dates the text to before the 2nd century BCE. This apocryphal manuscript contains Babylonian mythic material, but most of this book seems to have been based on the Book of Enoch. Aramaic versions were found among the Dead Sea Scrolls at Qumran and fragments and allusions to the Manichean version of the Book of the Giants, which were spread by the Manichean religion, have been found in medieval manuscripts in many languages. Among other things, the text relates how some giants had dreams foreseeing the deluge.

Reading the Ethiopic Book of Enoch 1-36 (the Book of Watchers) is strongly advised. According to the Ethiopic version of the Book of Enoch, thousands of years ago angels fell from heaven and made love with women. From this act a generation of giants were born. These giants taught humankind many arts, but also destroyed everything and were close to destroy humankind, when God asked Noah to build the Ark and sent the deluge, which killed all giants and fallen angels. According to one tradition one of the fallen angels, called Ohyah, survived the flood, but was killed later by archangel Raphael and Leviathan (when "they vanished") in a fight.

This book presents both the Manichean and the Dead Sea Scroll version. The Manichean version was extracted from the Bulletin of the School of Oriental and African Studies, University of London, Vol. XI, Part 1, first published in 1943, pp. 52-74. The transcriptions of the original texts have been omitted in this version. The Dead Sea Scroll version was discovered between 1946 and 1956 and were translated and published a few years later.

By Fabio R. Araujo, Historian. Author of *Prophezeiungen uber das Ende der Welt*, Kopp, 2009 (published in Spain as *Profecias sobre el fin de los tempos*, Edaf, 2013), a comparative study of myths, legends, and prophecies.

The Manichean Version

ISAAC DE BEAUSOBRE, the Huguenot author of one of the best books ever written on Manichæism (*Histoire critique de Manichée et du Manichéisme*, Amsterdam, 1734, 1739), was the one to make the only sound suggestions on the sources used by Mani for the compilation of his *Book of the Giants:* the *Book of Enoch*, and the Γραφὴ τῶν Γιγάντων which Kenan, a great-grandson of Noah, discovered lying in a field (vol. i, 429, n. 6). The latter work has been identified by Alfaric (*Les Écritures Manichéennes*, ii, 32) with a book whose contents are briefly indicated in the *Decretum Gelasianum*, p. 54, ll. 298-9 (ed. Dobschütz): *Liber de Ogia*[1] *nomine gigante qui post diluvium cum dracone ab hereticis pugnasse perhibetur apocryphus*. Of the *Book of Enoch*, which was composed in the Hebrew language in the second century B.C., only an Ethiopic version, a few Greek fragments, and some excerpts made by the Byzantine chronographer Georgius Syncellus survive.[2] Mani, who could hardly read the Hebrew, must have used an Aramaic edition based directly on the Hebrew text (see below, *Šhmyz'd*). He quotes mainly from the first part, which Georgius S. (p. 45, Fl.-R.) calls "the first book of Enoch on the Egrēgoroi", but shows himself acquainted also with the subsequent chapters.[3]

It is noteworthy that Mani, who was brought up and spent most of his life in a province of the Persian empire, and whose mother belonged to a famous Parthian family,[4] did not make any use of the Iranian mythological tradition. There can no longer be any doubt that the Iranian names of *Sām*, *Narīmān*, etc., that appear in the Persian and Sogdian versions of the *Book of the Giants*, did not figure in the original edition, written by Mani in the Syriac language.[5] His disciples, who, it is well known, were in the habit of translating every word of a text (including the names of months, deities, etc.), seen fit also to "translate" the names of the giants. Thus *Sām* is merely the translation of *Ohya*. However, they kept some of the original names (e.g. *Šhmyz'd*), and adapted some others (e.g. *Wrwgd'd*).[6]

The story of the fallen angels and their giant sons needed little adaptation to be fitted into Mani's system. Of course, the heavenly origin of the *B'nē-hā-Elōhīm*[7] of Genesis vi, 2, 4, the *Ἐγρήγοροι*, of the *Book of Enoch*, did not square with Mani's conviction that no evil could come from good. Therefore he transformed them into "demons", namely those demons that when the world was being constructed had been imprisoned in the skies under the supervision of the *Rex Honoris*. They rebelled and were recaptured, but two hundred of them escaped to the earth. Mani also used the term *Ἐγρήγοροι* (preserved in Coptic, see texts L, M, P, S), or rather *'yr* in Aramaic (once in a Middle Persian fragment, text D), but in Eastern sources they are mostly referred to as "demons" (Pers. *dyw'n*, Parth. *dyw'n* in T 6, Sogd. *δywt* in G, H 17, K 7, *cytyt* in E, *δywt ZY ykšyšt* in H. 16).

The puzzling clause of Genesis vi, 4: "The Nephilim were on the earth those days," was interpreted by Mani in this fashion: "when the Egrēgoroi descended, the animals, or proto-animals, were already in existence." Mani confused *nəfīlīm* with *nefäl* (*näfäl*) = *ἔκτρωμα*: see Nöldeke, *ZDMG.*, 43 (1889), 536, who rightly referred to the formula of abjuration

(*P.Gr.*, i, 1461) where the giants and the "abortions" are mentioned in one breath. In Manichæan parlance, "abortion" (cf. also MPers. *'bg'ng*, Sogd. *pš'q*) is synonymous with "animal".

We are therefore left with the *Gibbōrīm*, understood by Mani[8] as "giants". He probably used the equivalent Syriac word, *gabbārē* (*gnbr'*), which his disciples translated as γίγαντες, *al-jabābirah* in Arabic, MPers. and Parthian *k'w'n*, Sogd. *kwyšt* = *kawišt* (Sing. *qwy* , *kw'y* = *kawi*); cf. *Sb.P.A.W.*, 1934, 30. In Sasanian times the words derived from the Avestan *Kavi* were generally understood as "giant"; see Benveniste, *MO.*, xxvi, 214, and Polotsky in *Mir.Man.*, iii, 901. Thus M Pers. Parth. *k'w* is freely used in Manichæan texts, e.g. of the Father of Light (M 40), of solar deities, of leading Manichæans (both in *Mir. Man.* iii), also of the First Man and Ahriman[9] with reference to the First Battle (which therefore could have been described as a γιγαντομαχία).[10] However, the word *k'w* is applied only to men and such beings as are imagined anthropomorphous. Where one would translate γίγας as *monster*, the Iranian equivalent is *mzn*, *Mazan*. Thus the γίγας τῆς Θαλάσσης (*Kephalaia*, 113 and notes), whose breathing operations are responsible for ebb and flow (cf. also Beruni, *India*, 203, 10-11), is called *Mzn 'y (z)rhyg*[11] in Middle Persian (M 99, V 22-3). Accordingly, MPers. *mzn* (adj.[12] and noun) and the related words, Pahl. *mā zan, māzanīg,* Sogd. *mzny'n δyw,* Av. *māzainya-*,[13] should be rendered as "monster", or "gigantic, monstrous".

The Egrēgoroi and their giant progeny are fought and vanquished by four archangels: Raphael, Michael, Gabriel, and Istrael (*Enoch*, 10, 1; or: Uriel, or: Fanuel). In the *Book of the Giants* they are called "the four angels". They are frequently invoked by name in Manichæan prayers (e.g. M 4 d 19, f 6; M 20), as *Rwp'yl, Myx'yl, Gbr'yl,* and *Sr'yl* (= Istrael).

There were no details about individual feats of the giants in the *Book of Enoch*. Mani filled the gap with the help of the above-mentioned *Liber de Ogia nomine gigante*. This *Ogias* has been identified with *Og of Bashan*,[14] who according to late sources lived five thousand years and managed to survive the Deluge, thanks to his giant size.[15] But possibly stories that primarily appertained to *Ogias* were transferred to the better known *Og*, owing to the resemblance of their names. The name of *Ogias* is *'why'* (*'whַy*) = *Ohyā⸱* (*Oḥyā⸱*) in the Manichæan fragments, and this spelling is presumably more correct than that of *Ogias. Og* (*'wg*) indubitably would appear as *'wg* (or: *'wg*). Since Mani took *'why'* from an Aramaic text, the ending of *Ogias* cannot be regarded as a Greek addition.

Ogias fought with a *draco*, and so did Ohya; his enemy was the Leviathan (text N). Ohya and his brother Ahya were the sons of *Šhmyz'd* (text H), i.e. Στμαζᾶς, the chief of the Egrēgoroi in the *Book of Enoch*; hence, Στμαζᾶς is transcription of *šhm-* (or *šhm*?). In the Persian edition of the *Kawān* Ohya and Ahya are "translated" as *Sām* and *Narīmān*, but the original names are kept in one passage (A 60). The translator did well to choose Sām-Krsāsp, both with regard to Ogias' longevity (Sām is one of the "Immortals") and to his fight with the dragon (Sām is a famous dragon-killer). In the Sogdian fragments the name of Sām is spelt *S'hm* = *Sāhm*, as it is often in Pahlavi (*S'hm*[16] beside *S'm*); Ṭabari has *Shm*,[17] cf. Christensen, *Kayanides*, p. 130. Sāhm's brother is *Pāt-Sāhm*. This name may have been invented by the Sogdian translator in order to keep the names of the brothers resembling each other. Narīmān was evidently not known in Sogdiana as a brother of Sām. According to the *Book of the Giants*, the main preoccupation of Sām-Sāhm was his quarrel the giant *Māhawai*,[18] the son of *Virōgdād*, who was one of the twenty ers of the Egrēgoroi.

The Book of the Giants was published in not less than six or seven languages. From the original Syriac the Greek and Middle Persian versions were made. The Sogdian edition was probably derived from the Middle Persian, the Uygur from the Sogdian. There is no trace of a Parthian text.[19] The book may have existed in Coptic. The presence of names such as Sām and Narīmān in the Arabic version proves that it had been translated from the Middle Persian. To the few surviving fragments (texts A-G) I have added two excerpts, the more important of which (H) probably derives from a Syriac epitome of the book. Naturally, Manichæan authors quoted the book frequently, but there is only one direct citation by a non-Manichæan writer (text O). With the exception of text O, all the passages referring to the *Book of the Giants* (texts J-T) go back to Syriac writings (apparently). They are, therefore, to be treated as quotations from the Syriac edition. E.g. the

Parthian text N is not the product of a Parthian writer who might have employed a Parthian version of the book, but was translated from a Syriac treatise whose author cited the Syriac text.

In their journey across Central Asia the stories of the *Book of the Giants* were influenced by local traditions. Thus, the translation of Ohya as Sām had in its train the introduction of myths appertaining to that Iranian hero; this explains the "immortality" of Sā(h)m according to text I. The country of *Aryān-Vēžan = Airyana Vaējah*, in text G (26), is a similar innovation.[20] The "Kögmän mountains" in text B may reflect the "Mount Hermon". The progeny of the fallen angels was confined in thirty-six towns (text S). Owing to the introduction of the Mount Sumeru, this number was changed (in Sogdiana) to *thirty-two* (text G, 22): "the heaven of Indra ... is situated between the four peaks (cf. G 21) of the Meru, and consists of *thirty-two* cities of devas" (Eitel, *Handb. Chinese Buddhism*, 148, on *Trayastriṃśat*).

TEXTS

(bcd) = damaged letters, or uncertain readings.

[bcd] = suggested restorations of missing letters.

... = visible, but illegible letters.

[...] = estimated number of missing letters.

[ ] = a lacuna of undetermined extent.

(84)] = same, at the beginning of a line.

[(85 = same, at the end of a line.[21]

In the translation parentheses are employed for explanatory remarks.

FRAGMENTS OF THE KAWĀN

A. Middle-Persian

M 101, *a* to *n*, and M 911, fifteen fragments of a book, throughout small pieces from the centre of the pages. It has proved impossible, so far, to re-establish the original order of the pages. On purely technical grounds (size of the fragments, appearance of the margins, relative position of tears, stains, etc.), I at first assumed the following sequence: l-j-k-g-i-c-e-b-h-f-a-d-m-M 911-n. Being unable to estimate the cogency of these technical reasons now, because of the absence of any photographic material, I have decided to change the order of the first six fragments in the following way: c-j-l-k-g-i, in view of their contents.[22] Unfortunately we do not know in what order Mani had told the story of the giants. The task of finding the original order is made still more difficult by the fact that besides the *Kawān* the book contained one or two more treatises, namely: (1) Parables referring to the Hearers, and possibly (2) a discourse on the Five Elements (here (1) = lines 160 to the end, and (2) = lines 112-159). The only fragments that undoubtedly belonged to the *Kawān* are c-j-l-k-g-i, while the position of the fragments e-b-h is particularly doubtful. It must be borne in mind that whole folios may be missing between apparently successive pages. In order to enable the reader to judge for himself, all the fragments (including the parables) are published here. The text is based on a copy I made nearly ten years ago (referred to in the notes as: Copy); a revision is not possible under the present circumstances.

Translation

(*Frg. c*) . . . hard . . . arrow . . . bow, he that . . . Sām said: "Blessed be . . . had [he ?] seen this, he would not have died." Then Shahmīzād said to Sām, his [son]: "All that Māhawai . . ., is spoilt (?)." Thereupon he said to . . . "We are . . . until (10) . . . and . . . (13) . . . that are in (?) the fiery hell (?) . . . As my father, Virōgdād, was . . ." Shahmīzād said: "It is true what he says. He says one of thousands.[23] For one of thousands . . . .". Sām thereupon began . . . Māhawai, too, in many places . . . (20) until to that place he might escape (1) and . . .[24]

(*Frg. j*) . . . Virōgdād . . . Hōbābīš [25] robbed Ahr . . .[26] of -naxtag,[27] his wife. Thereupon the giants began to kill each other and [to abduct their wives]. The creatures, too, began to kill each other.[28] Sām . . . before the sun, one hand in the air, the other (30) . . . whatever he obtained, to his brother . . . . imprisoned . . . (34) . . . over Taxtag.[29] To the angels . . . from heaven. Taxtag to . . . Taxtag threw (*or:* was thrown) into the water. Finally (?) . . . in his sleep Taxtag saw three signs, [one portending . . .], one woe and flight, and one . . . annihilation. Narīmān saw a gar[den full of] (40) trees in rows. Two hundred . . . came out, the trees. . . . [30]

(*Frg. l*) . . . Enoch,[31] the apostle, . . . [gave] a message to [the demons and their] children: To you . . . not peace.[32] [The judgment on you is] that you shall be bound for the sins you have committed.[33] You shall see the destruction of your children.[34] ruling for a hundred and twenty[35] [years] . . . . (50) . . . wild ass, ibex . . . ram, goat (?),[36] gazelle, . . . oryx, of each two hundred, a pair[37] . . . the other wild beasts, birds, and animals and their wine [shall be] six thousand jugs . . . irritation(?)[38] of water (?) . . . and their oil shall be [39] . . .

(*Frg. k*) ... father ... nuptials (?) ... until the completion of his ... in fighting ... (60) ... and in the nest(?) Ohya and Ahya ... he said to his brother: "get up and ... we will take what our father has ordered us to. The pledge we have given ... battle." And the giants ... together ... (67) "[Not the] ... of the lion, but the ... on his ... [Not the] ... of the rainbow, but the bow ... firm. Not the sharpness of the blade, [but] (70) the strength of the ox (?).[40] Not the ... eagle, but his wings.[41] Not the ... gold, but the brass that hammers[42] it. Not the proud [ruler], but the diadem on his [head. Not] the splendid cypress, but the ... of the mountain ...

(*Frg. g*) ... Not he that engages in quarrels, but he that is true in his speech. Not the evil fruit(?), but the poison in it. (80) [Not they that] are placed (?) [43] in the skies but the God [of all] worlds. Not the servant is proud, but [the lord] that is above him. Not one that is sent ..., but the man that sent him".[44] Thereupon Narīmān ... said ... (86) ... And (in) another place I saw those that were weeping for the ruin that had befallen them, and whose cries and laments rose up to heaven. (90) And also I saw another place [where there were] tyrants and rulers ... in great number, who had lived [45] in sin and evil deeds, when [46] ...

(*Frg. i*) [47] ... many ... were killed, four hundred thousand Righteous [48] ... with fire, naphtha, and brimstone [49] ... And the angels veiled [50] (*or:* covered, *or:* protected, *or:* moved out of sight) Enoch. *Electae et auditrices* (100) ... and ravished them. They chose beautiful [women], and demanded ... them in marriage.[51] Sordid ... (103) ... all ... carried off ... severally they were subjected to tasks and services. And they ... from each city ... and were, ordered to serve the ... The Mesenians [were directed] to prepare, the Khūzians [52] to sweep [and] (110) water, the Persians to ...

[On the Five Elements]

(*Frg. e*) (112) ... slaying ... righteous ... good deeds .... elements. The crown, the diadem, [the garland, and] the garment (of Light). The seven demons. Like a blacksmith [who] binds (*or:* shuts, fastens) and looses (*or:* opens, detaches) .... who from the seeds of .... and serves the king .... (120) ... offends ... when weeping ... with mercy ... hand ... (125) ... the Pious gave ... ? ... presents. Some buried the idols. The Jews did good and evil. Some make their god half demon, half god . . . (130) killing . . . the seven demons . . . eye . . .

(*Frg. b*) . . . various colours that by . . . and bile. If. . . . from the five elements. As if (it were) a means not to die, they fill themselves with food and drink. Their (140) garment is . . . this corpse . . . and not firm . . . Its ground is not firm . . . Like . . . (146) . . . imprisoned [in this corpse], in bones, nerves,[53] [flesh], veins, and skin, and entered herself [= Āz] into it. Then he (= Man) cries out, over [54] (?) sun and moon, the Just God's (150) two flames [55] . . . ? . . .,[56] over the elements, the trees and the animals. But God [Zrwān ?], in each epoch,[57] sends apostles: Šīt[īl, Zarathushtra,] Buddha, Christ, . . .

(*Frg. h*) . . . evil-intentioned . . . from where . . . he came. The Misguided recognize the five elements, [the five kinds of] trees, the five (kinds of) animals.

(160) . . . On the Hearers

. . . we receive . . . from Mani, the Lord, . . . the Five Commandments to . . . the Three

Seals ... (164) ... living ... profession ... and wisdom ... moon. Rest from the power (*or*: deceit) ... own. And keep measured the mixture (?) ... trees and wells, in two ... (170) water, and fruit, milk, ... he should not offend his brother. The wise [Hearer] who like unto juniper [leaves [58] ...

(*Frg. f*) ... much profit. Like a farmer ... who sows seed .. in many [59] ... The Hearer who ... knowledge, is like unto a man that threw (the dish called)[60] *frōšag* (180) [into] milk(?). It became hard, not ... The part that ruin ... at first heavy. Like ... first ... is honoured ... might shine ... (188) six days. The Hearer who gives alms (to the Elect), is like unto a poor (190) man that presents his daughter to the king; he reaches (a position of) great honour.[61] In the body of the Elect the (food given to to him as) alms is purified in the same manner as a ... that by fire and wind ... beautiful clothes on a clean body ... turn ...

(*Frg. a*) ... witness ... fruit ... (200) ... tree ... like firewood ... like a grain (?) ... radiance. The Hearer in [the world ?], (and) the alms within the Church, are like unto a ship [on the sea] [62]: the towing-line [63] (is) in the hand of [the tower] on shore, the sailor (210) is [on board the ship]. The sea is the world, the ship is [the . . ., the . . . is the ?al]ms, the tower is [the . . . ?], the towing-line (?) is the Wisdom. . . . . . . (214) . . . The Hearer . . . is like unto the branch (?) of a fruitless [tree] . . . fruitless . . . and the Hearers . . . fruit that . . . (220) pious deeds. [The Elect,] the Hearer, and Vahman, are like unto three brothers to whom some [possessions] were left by their father: a piece of land, . . ., seed. They became partners . . . they reap and . . . The Hearer . . . like . . .

(*Frg. d*) . . . an image (?) of the king, cast of gold . . . (230) . . . the king gave presents. The Hearer that copies a book, is like unto a sick man that gave his . . . [64] to a . . . man. The Hearer that gives [his] daughter to the church,[65] is like . . . pledge, who (= father ?) gave his son to . . . learn . . . to . . . father, pledge . . . (240) . . . Hearer. Again, the Hearer . . . is like . . . . stumble . . . is purified. To . . . the soul from the Church, is like unto the wife of the soldier (*or*: Roman) who . . . infantrist, one shoe . . . who, however, with a denarius . . . was. The wind tore out one . . . he was abashed [66] . . . from the ground . . . ground . . .

(*Frg. m*) ... (250) ... sent ... The Hearer that makes one ..., is like unto [a compassionate mother] who had seven sons ... the enemy [killed] all ... The Hearer that ... piety ... (258) ... a well. One [on the shore of] the sea, one in the boat. (260) [He that is on] shore, tows(?) him that is [in the boat].[67] He that is in the boat. ... sea. Upwards to ... like .. ? .. like a pearl ... diadem ...

(*Frg. M* 911) ... Church. Like unto a man that ... fruit and flowers ... then they praise ... fruitful tree ... (270) ... [Like unto a man] that bought a piece of land. [On that] piece of land [there was] a well, [and in that well a bag] full of drachmas ... the king was filled with wonder ... share ... pledge ...

(*Frg. n*) ... numerous ... Hearer. At ... like unto a garment ... (280) like ... to the master ... like ... and a blacksmith. The goldsmith ... to honour, the blacksmith to ... one to ...

B. *Uygur*

LeCoq, *Türk. Man.*, iii, 23. Bang, *Muséon*, xliv, 13-17. Order of pages according to

LeCoq (the phot. publ. by Bang seems to support LeCoq's opinion).

(*First page*) . . . fire was going to come out. And [I saw] that the sun was at the point of rising, and that [his ?] centre (*orḍu*) without increasing (? *ašïlmatïn* ?) above was going to start rolling. Then came a voice from the air above. Calling me, it spoke thus: "Oh son of Virōgdād, your affairs are lamentable (?). More than this you shall [not] see. Do not die now prematurely, but turn quickly back from here." And again, besides this (voice), I heard the voice of Enoch, the apostle, from the south, without, however, seeing him at all. Speaking my name very lovingly, he called. And downwards from . . . then

(*Second page*) . . . " . . for the closed [68] door of the sun will open, the sun's light and heat will descend and set your wings alight. You will burn and die," said he. Having heard these words, I beat my wings and quickly flew down from the air. I looked back: Dawn had . . . ., with the light of the sun it had come to rise over the Kögmän mountains. And again a voice came from above. Bringing the command of Enoch, the apostle, it said: "I call you, Virōgdād, . . . I know . . . his direction . . . you

... you ... Now quickly ... people ... also ...

C. Sogdian

M 648. Small scrap from the centre of a page. Order of pages uncertain.

(*First page*) ... I shall see. Thereupon now S[āhm, the giant] was [very] angry, and laid hands on M[āhawai, the giant], with the intention: I shall ... and kill [you]. Then ... the other g[iants ...

(*Second page*) ... do not be afraid, for ... [Sā]hm, the giant, will want to [kill] you, but I shall not let him ... I myself shall damage ... Thereupon Māhawai, the g[iant], ... was satisfied ...

D. Middle-Persian

Published *Sb.P.A.W.*, 1934, p. 29.

... outside ... and ... left .... read the dream we have seen. Thereupon Enoch thus .... and the trees that came out, those are the

Egrēgoroi (*'yr*), and the giants that came out of the women. And ..... over ... pulled out ... over ...

E. Sogdian

T iii 282. Order of pages uncertain.

(*First page*) ... [when] they saw the apostle, ... before the apostle ... those demons that were [timid], were very, very glad at seeing the apostle. All of them assembled before him. Also, of those that were tyrants and criminals, they were [worried] and much afraid.[69] Then ...

(*Second page*) ... not to ... Thereupon those powerful demons spoke thus to the pious apostle [70]: If .... by us any (further) sin [will] not [be committed ?], my lord, why ? .... you have ... and weighty injunction[71] ...

F. Middle-Persian

T ii D ii 164. Six fragmentary columns, from the middle of a page. Order of columns uncertain. Instead of A///B///CDEF, it might have been: BCDEFA, or even CDEF///A///B.[72]

(*Col. A*) . . . poverty . . . [those who] harassed [73] the happiness of the Righteous, on that account they shall fall into eternal ruin and distress, into that Fire, the mother of all conflagrations and the foundation of all ruined tyrants. And when these sinful misbegotten sons [74] of ruin in those crevices and . . . .

(*Col. B*) . . . you have not been better. In error you thought you would this false power eternally.[75] You . . . all this iniquity . . .

(*Col. C*) . . . you that call to us with the voice of falsehood. Neither did we reveal ourselves on *your* account, so that *you* could see us, nor thus . . . . ourselves through the praise and greatness that to us . . . ⁻given to you . . ., but . . .

(*Col. D*) . . . sinners . . . . . is visible, where out of this fire your soul will be prepared (for the transfer) to eternal ruin (?). And as for you, sinful misbegotten sons of the Wrathful Self,[76] confounders of the true words of that Holy One, disturbers of the actions of Good Deed, aggressors upon Piety, . . . ⁻ers of the Living. . . ., who their . . .

(*Col. E*) . . . and on brilliant wings they shall fly and soar further outside and above that Fire, and shall gaze into its depth and height. And those Righteous that will stand around it, outside and above, they themselves shall have power over that Great Fire, and over everything in it. . . . . . blaze . . . . souls that . . .

(*Col. F*) . . . they are purer and stronger [than the] Great Fire of Ruin that sets the worlds ablaze. They shall stand around it, outside and above, and splendour shall shine over them. Further outside and above it they shall fly [77] (?) after those souls that may try to escape from the Fire. And that . . . .

G. Sogdian

T ii. Two folios (one only publ. here; the other contains a *wyδβ'y cn pš'qt δywtyy* "Discourse on the Nephīlīm-demons"). Head-lines: *R: pš'n prβ'r* [78] ". . . pronouncement", *V: iv fryštyt δn CC* "The four angels with the two hundred [demons . . . ".

. . . they took and imprisoned all the helpers that were in the heavens. And the angels themselves descended from the heaven to the earth. And (when) the two hundred demons saw those angels, they were much afraid and worried. They assumed the shape of men [79] and hid themselves. Thereupon the angels forcibly removed the men [80] from the demons, (10) laid them aside, and put watchers over them . . . . the giants . . . . were sons . . . with each other in bodily union . . . . with each other self- . . . . and the . . . . that had been born to them, they forcibly removed them [81] from the demons. And they led one half of them (20) eastwards, and the other half westwards, on the skirts of four huge mountains, towards the foot of the Sumeru mountain, into thirty-two towns which the Living Spirit had prepared for them in the beginning.[82] And one calls (that place) Aryān-waižan. And those men are (*or:* were) . . . . in the first arts and crafts.[83] (30) . . . . they made . . . the angels . . . and to the demons . . . they went to fight. And those two hundred demons fought a hard battle with the [four angels], until [the angels used] fire, naphtha, and brimstone [84] . . . .

EXCERPTS

H. Sogdian

T ii S 20. Sogdian script.[85] Two folios. Contents similar to the "Kephalaia". Only about a quarter (I R i-17) publ. here. The following chapter has as headline: *"yšt š'nš'y cnn 'β[c'n]pδ[yh w]prs* = Here begins: Šanšai's [86] question the world. Init. *rty tym ZK š'nš'[y] [cnn] m'rm'ny rwyšny pr'yš[t'kw w'nkw ']prs' 'yn'k 'βc'npδ ZY kw ZKh mrtymyt ('skw'nt)* oo *ckn'c pyδ'r "zy mrch 'zyyr'nt* = And again Šanšai asked the Light Apostle: this world where mankind lives, why does one call it birth-death (*saṃsāra*, Chin. *shêng-szŭ*).

. . . and what they had seen in the heavens among the gods, and also what they had seen in hell, their native land, and furthermore what they had seen on earth,—all that they began to teach (*hendiadys*) to the men.[87] To Šahmīzād two(?) sons were borne by . . . . One of them he named "Ohya"; in Sogdian he is called "Sāhm, the giant". And again a second son [was born] to him. He named him "Ahya"; its Sogdian (equivalent) is "Pāt-Sāhm". As for the remaining giants, they were born to the other demons and Yakṣas. (*Colophon*) Completed:

(the chapter on) "The Coming of the two hundred Demons".

I. Sogdian

M 500 n. Small fragment.

.... manliness, in powerful tyranny, he (*or:* you ?) shall not die". The giant Sāhm and his brother will live eternally. For in the whole world in power and strength, and in .... [they have no equal].

QUOTATIONS AND ALLUSIONS

J. Middle-Persian

T ii D ii 120, V ii 1-5: and in the coming of the two hundred demons there are two paths: the hurting speech, and the hard labour; these (belong, *or:* lead) to hell.

K. Sogdian

M 363.

(*First page*) ... before ... they were. And all the ...[88] fulfilled their tasks lawfully. Now, they became excited and irritated for the following reason: namely, the two hundred demons came down to the sphere from the high heaven, and the . . . .

(*Second page*) . . . in the world they became excited and irritated. For their life-lines and the connections of their Pneumatic Veins [89] are joined to sphere. (*Colophon*) Completed: the exposition of the three worlds. (*Head-line*) Here begins: the coming of Jesus and [his bringing] the religion to Adam and Šitil. . . . you should care and . . .

L. Coptic

Kephalaia, 171^{16-19}: Earthquake and malice happened in the watchpost of the Great King of Honour, namely the Egrēgoroi who arose at the time when they were . . . . and there descended those who were sent to confound them.

M. Coptic

Kephalaia, 92^{24-31}: Now attend and behold how the Great King of Honour who is ἔννοια, is in the third heaven. He is . . . with the wrath . . . and a rebellion . . ., when malice and wrath arose in his camp, namely the Egrēgoroi of Heaven who in his watch-district (rebelled and) descended to the earth. They did all deeds of malice. They revealed the arts in the world, and the mysteries of heaven to the men. Rebellion and ruin came about on the earth . . .

N. Parthian

M 35, lines 21–36. Fragment of a treatise entitled *'rdhng wyfr's* = Commentary on (Mani's opus) *Ārdahang*.[90]

And the story about the Great Fire: like unto (the way in which) the Fire, with powerful wrath, swallows this world and enjoys it; like unto (the way in which) this fire that is in the body, swallows the exterior fire that is (*lit.* comes) in fruit and food, and enjoys it. Again, like unto (the story in which) two brothers who found a treasure, and a pursuer lacerated each other, and they died; like unto (the fight in which) Ohya, Lewyātīn (= Leviathan), and Raphael lacerated each other, and they vanished; like unto (the story in which) a lion cub, a calf in a wood (*or:* on a meadow), and a fox lacerated each other, [and they vanished, *or:* died]. Thus [the Great Fire swallows, etc.] both of the fires. . . .[91]

M 740. Another copy of this text.

O. Arabic, from Middle-Persian ? [92]

Al-Ghaḍanfar (Abū Isḥāq Ibr. b. Muḥ. al-Tibrīzī, middle of thirteenth century), in Sachau's edition of Beruni's *Āthār al-bāqiyah*, Intr., p. xiv: The *Book of the Giants*, by Mani of Babylon, is filled with stories about these (antediluvian) giants, amongst whom Sām and Narīmān.

P. Coptic

Keph. 93^{23-28}: On account of the malice and rebellion that had arisen in the watch-post of the Great King of Honour, namely the Egrēgoroi who from the heavens had descended to the earth,—on their account the four angels received their orders: they bound the Egrēgoroi with eternal fetters in the prison of the Dark(?), their sons were destroyed upon the earth.

Q. Coptic

Manich. Psalm-book, ed. Allberry, 142^{7-9}: The Righteous who were burnt in the fire, they endured. This multitude that were wiped out, four thousand . . . . Enoch also, the Sage, the transgressors being . . .

R. Coptic

Man. Homil., ed. Polotsky, 68^{18-19}: ... evil. 400,000 Righteous .... the years of Enoch ...

S. Coptic

Keph., 117^{1-9}: Before the Egrēgoroi rebelled and descended from heaven, a prison had been built for them in the depth of the earth beneath the mountains. Before the sons of the giants were born who knew not Righteousness and Piety among themselves, thirty-six towns had been prepared and erected, so that the sons of the giants should live in them, they that come to beget .... who live a thousand years.

T. Parthian

291^a. Order of pages unknown.

(*First page*) ... mirror ... image. ... distributed. The men ... and Enoch was veiled (= moved out of sight).[93] They took ... Afterwards, with donkey-goads .... slaves,[94] and waterless trees (?). Then ... and imprisoned the demons. And of them .... seven and twelve.

(*Second page*) . . . three thousand two hundred and eighty-[95] . . . the beginning of King Vištāsp.[96] . . . . in the palace he flamed forth (*or:* in the brilliant palace). And at night . . ., then to the broken gate . . . men . . . physicians, merchants, farmers, . . . at sea. ? . . . armoured he came out . . .

APPENDIX

U. Parthian

T ii D 58. From the end (. . . *r š t*) of a hymn.

. . . gifts. A peaceful sovereign [was] King Vištāsp, [in Aryā]n-Waižan[97]; Wahman and Zarēl . . . . The sovereign's queen, Khudōs,[98] received the Faith,[99] the prince . . . They have secured (a place in) the (heavenly) hall, and quietude for ever and ever . . .

V. Sogdian

M 692. Small fragment. Order of pages uncertain.

(*First page*) . . . because . . . the House of the Gods, eternal joy, and good . . ? . .[100] For so it is said: at that time . . . Yima was . . . in the world. And at the time of the new moon (?) . . . . the blessed denizens of the world [101] . . . all assembled [102] . . . all . . .

(*Second page*) . . . they offered five garlands in homage.[103] And Yima accepted those garlands . . . And those . . . that . . . . and great kingship . . . was his. And on . . . them . . . . And acclamations [104] . . . And from that pious (?) . . . he placed the garlands on his head . . . the denizens of the world . . .

Footnotes

<u>1</u> Numerous variants (p. 126, Dobschütz), e.g. *de ogiae, de oggie, diogiae, diogine, diogenes, de ozia, de ugia, de ugica, de ogiga, de eugia, de uegia, de eugenia,* etc. In Migne's *Patrologia Latina* the text is in vol. 59, 162-3.

<u>2</u> See Charles, *The Book of Enoch*, 2nd ed., 1912. For the Greek fragments (and Georgius S.) the edition by Flemming and Radermacher (= *Fl.-R.*) is quoted here. For Mani's use of the Enoch literature see my papers in *Sb.P.A.W.*, 1934, 27-32, and in *ZDMG.*, 90, 2-4.

<u>3</u> See below A 86-94, and compare G 19-21 with *Enoch* 67, 4, and G 38 with *Enoch* 17, 1; 21, 7; 54, 6; 67, 4-13. On chaps. 72 sqq. see *Sb.P.A.W.*, 1934, 32.

<u>4</u> Namely the *Kamsarakan-k'* (mentioned often in the Armenian history of the fourth century) who claimed descent from the royal house of the Arsacids. This is clear from the Chinese-Manichæan text that preceded the *Fragment Pelliot*, now printed in the Taishô Tripiṭaka as No. 2141a, vol. 54, p. 1280A, but hitherto untranslated: "He was born in the country of Sulin (= Babylonia), in the royal abode

of *B'uât-tiei* (= *Patī-g*), by his wife *Muân-i͟ äm* (= *Maryam*) of the family of *Ki͟ əm-sât-g'i͟ ᴅn* (= *Kamsar(a)gān*)." The name Κάρασσα in the Byzantine formula of abjuration (Migne, *Patr. Gr.*, i, 1468) may be corrupted from *Kamsar-*. Thus there is a grain of truth in the assertion in the *K. al-Fihrist*, 327, 31, that Mani's mother had belonged to the Arsacid house; ibid., *Maryam* (ed, *marmaryam*) is given as one of her names.—It is not proposed to discuss the origin of Mani's father here.

<u>5</u> I have abandoned my earlier opinion on this point (*ZDMG.*, 90, 4) which was based on insufficient material. The important Sogdian fragment, text H, was not then known to me.

<u>6</u> See *BSOS.*, viii, 583; *ZDMG.*, 90, 4. [Cf. also Bal. *girōk*, Geiger, No.107.]

<u>7</u> Cf. also Parthian *bgpwhr'n*, Sogd. *βγpšyt*, lit. "sons of God" = angels (also fem. Sogd. *βγpwryšt*). Thus *bgpwhr* has a double meaning in Parthian, it being (Sogd. *βγpwr*) also the translation of Chin. *T'ien-tzŭ*, or rather of Skt. *devaputra*.

<u>8</u> Herein he differed from the common interpretation of the passage (Nephilim =

giants), shared also by the authors of the *Book of Enoch*.

<u>9</u> M 41: *'br q'rc'r 'wt̲ zmbg 'stft cy 'whrmyzdbg qyrd 'd dyw'n: dw q'w'n 'wt̲ dw nyw'n.*

<u>10</u> This word, in the anti-Manichæan book by Alexander Lycopolitanus, p. 8, 10, ed. Brinkmann, refers neither to the Manich. "First Battle", nor to Mani's *Book of the Giants*, as Cumont, *Rech.*, i, 3; ii, 160 sq., erroneously states. Cumont goes so far as to say that in the quoted passage Alexander had given a summary of Mani's work, and Benveniste, *MO.*, xxvi, 213, has repeated this statement. In fact, Alexander says that experts in Greek mythology might quote, from the Greek poets, the *Greek γιγαντομαχία, as a parallel* to the Manich. doctrine of the rising by the Hyle against God. In ch. 25 (p. 37, 13 sqq.) Alexander explains that such poetical fables about giants could not be regarded as a satisfactory parallel, because they were myths and meant to be understood as allegories. He then (37, 17) quotes the story of *Genesis* vi, 2-4, which he provides with an allegorical explanation. But he ascribes it to the *History of the Jews* without even mentioning the *Book*

of the Giants. This shows conclusively that he had no knowledge of Mani's book.

11 Jackson, *Researches*, 37, 67 sq., has "poisonous mass"; cf. *OLZ.*, 1934, 752.

12 Hence the comparative *mzndr* (e.g. *Mir.Man.*, i) and the superlative Pahl. *mā ̆zan-tum* (e.g. *Dd.*, p. 118, 12 ed. Anklesaria).

13 Clearly to be derived from Av. *mazan-* "greatness". Cf. also Jackson, loc. cit., on *mzn*. Hence, the first part of the name of *Māzandarān* probably = "gigantic".

14 Thus Dobschütz, *Decret. Gelas.*, p. 305.

15 Dobschütz, loc. cit., who quotes Fabricius, *Cod. pseudepigr.*, 799 sq., and Migne, *Dict. des apocr.*, ii, 649, 1295.

16 For example, *Men.Khr.*, 68, 12; 69, 12, ed. Andreas; *Pahl. Yasna*, 9, 10 (p. 71, 19).

17 *Shm*, of course, transcribes *S'hm*, not *S'm*.

18 MPers. *m'hw'y* A 7, with suff. *m'hwy-c* A 19, Sogd. *m'h'wy* C 15 (= *Wrogdad oɣlï* in B). Hardly = *Māhōi* (as suggested *ZDMG.*, 90, 4), for the ending *-ōi* was pronounced *-ōi* also in

the third century (cf. e.g. *wyrwd* = *Wērōi* in the inscription of Shapur, line 34). Furthermore, there was no Māhōi among the heroes of the Iranian epos (M. is well known as the name of the governor of Marv at the time of the last Yezdegerd). More likely *Māhawai* was a non-Iranian name and figured already in the Aramaic edition of the *Kawān*; it may have been adapted to Persian. Cf. *Mḥwy'l*, Genesis, iv, 18 ?

19 But see *Mir.Man.*, iii, 858 (b 134 sqq.).

20 The children of the Egrēgoroi share with the inhabitants of Airyana Vaējah the distinction of being regarded as the inventors (or first users) of the arts and crafts. For the spelling of *Aryān-Vēžan* see also Appendix, text U. It is not clear whether *Yima* (text V) had been given a place in the Sogdian *Kawān*. *Ymyẖ*, i.e. *Imi*, is the correct Sogdian form of the name.

21 This system of notation has been used also in my book *Sogdica*, and in my paper in *BSOS.*, X, pp. 941 sqq. The various interpunction marks are uniformly represented by oo here.

22 But possibly *Frg. i* should occupy the first place; see below, notes on lines 95–111.

23 = far less than he could say. Cf. *əž hazār yak*, *ŠGV.*, xiv, 2, *əž hazārą baewarą yak*, ibid., xvi, 1. Salemann, *Zap. Imp. Ak. Nauk, sér. viii, t. vi, No.* 6, 25, quoted Persian *az hazār yakī va az bisyār andakī*.

24 The texts *B* and *C* (Uygur and Sogdian) could be inserted here (or hereabouts).

25 Probably one of the twenty "decarchs" (*Enoch* 6, 7), viz. No. 4 *Kokabiel* = Χωχαριήλ in the Greek fragments, and Χωβαβιήλ apud Syncellus.

26 This also could be a "decarch", *Arakib*- Ἀρακιήλ, or *Aramiel*- Ῥαμιήλ.

27 Incomplete name.

28 Cf. Enoch 7, 5.

29 *txtg* might be appellative, = "a board". This would fit in three of the passages, but hardly in the fourth.

30 Evidently this is the dream that Enoch reads in the fragment M 625c (= Text D, below), which therefore probably belonged to the *Kawān*. It should be inserted here.

31 Here (or hereabouts) the texts E and F should be entered, both of which deal with the judgment on the fallen angels. Text F approximates to *Enoch*, ch. 10 (pronouncement of the judgment by God), while Text E is nearer to *Enoch*, ch. 13 (communication of the judgment the angels by Enoch).

32 = *Enoch*, 12, 4-5: εἰπὲ τοῖς ἐγρηγόροις . . . . οὐκ ἔσται ὑμῖν εἰρήνη.

33 = *Enoch*, 13, 1-2: ὁ δὲ ’Ενώχ . . . εἶπεν . . . οὐκ ἔσται σοι εἰρήνη κρῖμα μέγα ἐξῆλθεν κατὰ σοῦ δῆσαί σε . . . περί . . . τῆς ἀδικίας καὶ τῆς ἁμαρτίας κτλ.

34 = *Enoch*, 14, 6: ἴδητε τὴν ἀπώλειαν τῶν υἱῶν ὑμῶν.

35 = Syncellus, pp. 44-5 Fl.-R. (*ad cap.* xvi), cf. *Genesis*, vi, 3. ἀπολοῦνται οἱ ἀγαπητοὶ ὑμῶν . . . . ὅτι πᾶσαι αἱ ἡμέραι τῆς ζωῆς αὐτῶν ἀπὸ τοῦ νῦν οὐ μὴ ἔσονται πλείω τῶν ἑκατὸν εἴκοσιν ἐτῶν.

36 In Jewish Persian *trwš* is "ram" (Lagarde, *Pers. Stud.*, 73), but in the dialect of Rīšahr nr. Bushire (according to the notes made on this dialect by Andreas about seventy years ago) tîštär is "a young she-goat".

See *JRAS.*, 1942, 248. [*trwš*, Is. 1^{11}, Ier. 51^{40} = Hebr. ʿattūd, probably understood as "he-goat".]

<u>37</u> These lines evidently refer to the promise of peace and plenty that concludes the divine judgment in *Enoch*, 10. Hence = "each pair of those animals shall have two hundred young"?

<u>38</u> *sārišn*: cf. *DkM.* 487 *apu.*-488, 3, "when they provoke (*sārēn-*) him he does not get irritated (*sār-* and better, *sārih-*)." *GrBd.* 5, 8, "if you do not provoke, or instigate (*sārēn-*) a fight" (differently Nyberg, ii, 202). *sār-*, if from *sarəd-* (Skt. *śardh-*), is presumably the transitive to *syrydn* (from *srdhya-* according to Bartholomæ), cf. *NGGW.*, 1932, 215, n. 3.

<u>39</u> Cf. *Enoch*, 10, 19: ἡ ἄμπελος [sic] ἣν ἂν φυτεύσωσιν ποιήσουσιν πρόχους οἴνου χιλιάδας . . . . ἐλαίας . . . .

<u>40</u> *ty* or *ty*[*y*]
= *tai* from *taih* from *taiɣ* (cf. *GGA.*, 1935, 18), is ambiguous: (1) sharp instrument, (2) burning, glow, brightness, sunrays, etc. So also is *tyzyy*: (1) sharpness, (2) speed. One could also restore *ty*[*gr*].

41 Lit. "but the Wing(s) that (is, are) with him." The curious expression was chosen probably on account of the rhythm. For the same reason *byc* is employed in the place of *'n'y* in line 73.

42 Lit. "beats".

43 *'ystyh-* is obviously different from *'styh-* (on which see *BSOS.*, IX, 81), and possibly derived from *'yst-*, cf. *z'yh-* "to be born" from *z'y-* "to be born". *'ystyh-* is met with in *W.-L.*, ii, 558, R i 25, "blessed chief who stands (*'ystyhyd*?) as the sign of the Light Gods." Lentz has *'ystyhnd*, but without having seen the manuscript one may presume a misreading (cf. ibid., R i 1, Lentz: *pd*[. .]*dg*, but probably *pr*[*'d*]*ng*, R i 2, Lentz: *p.d'r*, but probably *pyr'r*, ibid., R ii 22, Lentz: *'n.z*, but probably *''wn*; for further cases see *OLZ.*, 1934, 10).

44 St. John, 13, 18.

45 *phrystn: phryz-* = Parth. *prx'štn: prxyz-* (cf. Av. *pārihaēza-*, Sogd. *pr-γyž*; Parth. *'x'št:* MPers. *'xyst*) is mostly "to stand around, to be about, *versari*", sometimes "to stand around for the purpose of looking after someone" = "serve, nurse, protect", often merely "to

be". *phryz-* "to stand off, to abstain" is presumably different (*para-haēza-*).

<u>46</u> The series of visions in which Enoch sees the arrangements for the punishment of the fallen angels, etc., and of "the kings and the Mighty" (chaps. xvii sqq.), follows immediately upon the announcement of the divine judgment. Hence, frgg. *k-g* must be placed after frg. l. Text G (below), which describes, the execution of the divine order, could perhaps be inserted here.

<u>47</u> It is difficult to decide whether this fragment should be placed at the end or at the beginning of the book. The 400,000 Righteous may have perished when the Egrēgoroi descended to the earth. The "choosing of beautiful women", etc., strongly suggests the misbehaviour of the Egrēgoroi on their arrival upon the earth. The hard labour imposed on the Mesenians and other nations may be due to the insatiable needs of their giant progeny (*Enoch*, 7, 2 sqq.). On the other hand, "fire, naphtha, and brimstone" are only mentioned as the weapons with which the archangels overcame the Egrēgoroi, after a prolonged and heavy fight (Text G, 38), and the 400,000 Righteous may well have been the innocent

non-combatant victims of this battle which may have had a demoralizing effect even upon the *electae*. To clear up the debris the archangels would naturally commandeer the men. We do not know whether Mani believed Enoch to have been moved out of sight (ἐλήμφθη *Enoch*, 12, 1) before the Egrēgoroi appeared, or before they were punished.

48 See texts R, and Q (where 4,000 instead of 400,000).

49 See *BSOS.*, X, 398.

50 See text T, line 3.

51 Cf. *Enoch*, 7, 1 ?

52 On *myšn'yg'n* see *BSOS.*, X, 945, n. 2, on *hwjyg*, ibid., 944, n. 7.

53 *py(y)* always = nerves, sinews (not "fat" as in *Mir.Man.*, i, etc., as alternative rendering). It is equivalent to *nerfs* (Chavannes-Pelliot, *Traité Man.*, 32/3 [528/9]), Uygur *singir* (*T.M.*, iii, 18/9), Copt. = *Sehne*(*Keph.*, 96, etc.), Sogd. *pδδw'* (unpubl.). Cf. also *GrBd.*, 196, 4, where Goetze, *ZII.*, ii, 70, wrongly has "fat".

MPers. *pai* = NPers. *pai* = Pashto *pala* = Sogd. *pδδw'* (not Av. *piθwā-*).

54 Hardly "to". Cf. Cumont, *Rech.*, i, 49, and my paper *NGGW.*, 1932, 224.

55 Or: over the Just God, sun and moon, the (*or:* his) two flames. The "Just God" is the Messenger (not = *bgr'štygr*, i.e. Zrwān).

56 Unintelligible. Lit. ". . . two flames given into the (*or:* his) hand".

57 Cf. *Sb.P.A.W.*, 1934, 27, and *BSOS.*, VIII, 585.

58 Cf. M 171, 32 sqq. *'wṯ 'st ngwš'g ky 'w 'b[w](r)[s] m'nh'g ky hmyw zrgwng 'štyd 'wš zmg 'wd t'b'n png ny ryzynd. 'w'gwn hwyc hwrw'n ngwš'g pd pzd 'wd wšyd'x pd xw'r 'wṯ dyjw'r, kd dwr 'c wjydg'n 'wṯ kd nzd 'w wjydg'n, hw pd wxybyy frhyft 'wd w'wryft 'škbyd*, etc. "And some Hearers are like unto the juniper which is ever green, and whose leaves are shed neither in summer nor in winter. So also the pious Hearer, in times of persecution and of free exercise (lit. open-mindedness), in good and bad days, under the eyes of the Elect or out of their sight,—he is constant in his charity and faith." Although the

word *'brws* is incomplete in both passages, its restoration is practically a certainty.

<u>59</u> Possibly the parable of St. Mark, iv, 3 sqq.

<u>60</u> *BSOS.*, IX, 86.

<u>61</u> An elaborate version of this parable is found in M 221 R 9-23: *u nywš'g ky h'n rw'ng'n 'w wjyydg'n "wryyd, "wn m'n'g c'wn 'škwẖ myrd [ky] dwxt 'y nyq z'd hy, 'wd pd wryhryy 'wd 'gr'yyẖ 'byr hwcyyhr hy. 'wd h'n myrd 'y 'škwẖ 'w hwcyhryyẖ 'y 'wy qnyycg xwyš dwxtr prg' myyẖ cy 'byr h[wcyhr] [h]y. 'wd 'wy dwxtr 'y hwcyhr [   ]. 'wš 'w šẖ hndyym'n [qwnyẖ] 'wd šẖ 'wy qnycg ps[ndyẖ ?] 'wd pd znyy nš'yy. 'wš [   ] pws 'cyyš z'ynd[   ] pwsryn 'yš 'c 'w[y myrd 'y 'š]kwẖ dwxtr z['d* (remainder missing), "The Hearer that brings alms to the Elect, is like unto a poor man to whom a pretty daughter has been born, who is very beautiful with charm and loveliness. That poor man fosters the beauty of that girl, his daughter, for she is very beautiful. And that beautiful daughter, he presents her to the king. The king approves of her, and puts her into his harem. He has [several] sons by her. The sons that were born to that poor man's daughter . . . .".

Throughout the story the *parabolic optative* is in use.

<u>62</u> For a similar parable see below, lines 258 sqq.

<u>63</u> *zyyg*: this word, hitherto unexplained, occurs in the *Šābuhragān* (M 470 V 14, spelt *z'yg*). The sinners, roasting in hell, see the Righteous enjoying the New Paradise, and ask them: ... *'wm'n ... z'yg 'w dst dyy[d 'wd]c 'yn swcyšn bwzy[d]* "... put a rope (*or*: life-line) in our hands and rescue us from this conflagration". Cf. Pahl., Pers. *zīg*, Nyberg, *Mazd. Kal.*, 68.

<u>64</u> Possibly "weapons".

<u>65</u> Cf. *Kephalaia*, 192/3.

<u>66</u> Cf. *āhīd-gar-ān* below, F 43/4. For a discussion of *āhīd* see Zaehner; *BSOS.*, IX, 315 sq. Perhaps one can understand Av. *āhiti-* as "something that causes shame", hence "stain", etc. In that case *Anāhitā* could be compared to *Apsaras*. As regards NPers. *xīre*, mentioned by Zaehner, this may be connected with Sogd. *γyr'k* "foolish". The word in *DkM.*, 205^8, is not necessarily *hyrg-gwn* (thus Zaehner,

ibid., 312). It might be *hyl-* = Pashto *xər* "ashen, grey, etc."

<u>67</u> Cf. *supra*, lines 206-212.

<u>68</u> On *boɣuq* see Bang, loc. cit., p. 15, who has: "the door of the closed (locked) sun." Acc. to *Enoch*, chaps. 72 sqq., there are 180 doors in the east one of which is opened each morning for the sun to pass through (the idea, familiar also from Pahlavi books, is of Babylonian origin).

<u>69</u> Cf. *Enoch*, 13, 9, ἦλθον πρὸς αὐτούς, καὶ πάντες συνηγμένοι ἐκάθηντο πενθοῦντες κτλ.

<u>70</u> Cf. *Enoch*, 13, 4-6.

<u>71</u> i.e. the divine order for their punishment (*Enoch*, 10).

<u>72</u> [Other fragments of the same manuscript ("T i"), not however belonging to the *Kawān*, show that there were three columns to a page; hence, the correct order of the columns is: BCDEFA. Perhaps this text, too, is not a fragment of the *Kawān*.]

73 *murzīdan* is "persecute, harass", not "show pity" as hitherto translated (*S* 9; *Mir.Man.*, ii; *W.-L.*, ii, 556, r 6).

74 *ghwd* (*Mir.Man.*, ii), *ghwdg'n* (*Mir.Man.*, i), *ghwyn-* (*ZII.*, ix, 183, 27): the derivation of these words from *vi* + *hū* by Schaeder, *Sb.P.A.W.*, 1935, 492, n. 3, is based on the translation I had given; this translation, however, was based on nothing but this selfsame etymology.

75 *Enoch*, 10, 10.

76 This passage in particular seems to show that the text is a fragment of the *Kawān*. There are two groups of sinners here: one is (apparently) to be transferred from a preliminary fire-prison to the permanent hell at the end of the world (= the Egrēgoroi), the other consists of the κίβδηλοι (= Giants). The digression on their final fate in the great conflagration, under the eyes of the self-satisfied Righteous (cf. *Šābuhragān*, *M* 470 V), is well in keeping with Mani's discursive style.

77 *w'y-* (different from Parth. *w'y-* "to lead") = "to fly" or "to hunt" ? Cf. *w'ywg* "hunter" (*BBB.*, where the translation should be changed), *Air. Wb.* 1356, 1407.

78 My pupil I. Gershevitch thinks *prβ'r* should be derived from *prβyr-*. It is true that "explanation, announcement" fits most passages better than "chariot"! Hence, Mahāyāna rendered as "the great announcement" ?

79 *Enoch*, 17,1: ὅταν θέλωσιν φαίνονται ὡσεὶ ἄνθρωποι. *pts'δ*, cf. Skt. *praticchanda-*.

80 viz. the human associates of the demons, esp. the "daughters of men".

81 viz. the giants and their children ? Or merely the children of the giants ? See below, *S.* to Syncellus (*apud Fl.-R.*, p. 25) there were three generations: (1) the giants, (2) the Nephīlīm, their sons, and (3) the Eliud, their grandsons. In the *Book of Enoch* the giants are killed, or rather incited to kill each other, before the Egrēgoroi are punished (ch. 10). Their spirits shall roam the world, until the day of judgement, as πνεύματα πονηρά (15,8-16,1).

82 This passage shows that the Sogdian text had been translated from either Middle-Persian or Parthian (MPers. *ky myhryzd 'c nwx 'wyš'n r'y wyn'rd bwd*, Parthian *ky w'd jywndg 'c nwx hwyn wsn'd wyr'št bwd*).

83 'nδyk probably = skill, art, ability (differently, *BBB.*, p. 105).

84 See above, A 97.

85 Fairly cursive, difficult to read.

86 Probably by assimilation from *Šamšai* (= *Šimšai* in *Ezra*).

87 See above, G 28-9, and below, text M. According to *Enoch*, ch. 8, the fallen angels imparted to mankind unholy arts and undesirable knowledge, e.g. astrology, cosmetics, soothsaying, metallurgy, production of weapons, even the art of writing (ch. 69, 9).

88 Presumably the stellar demons.

89 Cf. *JRAS.* 1942, 232 n. 6.

90 If Mani's famous *Ertenk* was indeed a picture-book, this *Vifrās* may well have been the explanatory text published together with it; cf. Polotsky's suggestion, *Man. Hom.*, 18, n. 1, on Mani's εἰκών (but see *BBB.*, pp. 9 sq.). There is no reason for "identifying" the *Ertenk* with Mani's *Evangelion* (Schaeder, *Gnomon*, 9, 347). The fragments of the *Vifrās* (M 35, M 186, M

205, M 258, M 740, T ii K, T iii D 278) will be published at some other opportunity.

91 The point is that A eats or kills B, after B had finished C. A man killed his brother over the treaaure, but was killed by a third party, etc. The Great Fire will devour the bodily fire which had swallowed the "exterior fire". Hence, Ohya killed Leviathan, but was killed by Raphael.

92 St. Wikander, *Vayu*, i [1941], 166, quotes my article on Enoch, and my paper in *ZDMG.*, 1936, p. 4, and remarks
that *eigentuemlicherweise* I had forgotten Al-Ghaḍanfar's notice on Sām and Narīmān. Less careless readers will find Ghaḍanfar's notice quoted *in extenso* on the page cited by Wikander.

93 See above, A 98.

94 Cf. above. A 105 sqq.

95 Presumably the number of years supposed to have passed from the time of Enoch to the beginning of the reign of Vištāsp. The date for Enoch was probably calculated with the help of the Jewish world-era, or the mundane era of Alexandria (beginning 5493 B.C.), or by

counting backwards from the Deluge. Taking 3237 B.C. (but 3251 B.C. according to the Coptic chronology) as the date of the Deluge (see S. H. Taqizadeh, *BSOS.*, X, 122, under *c*), and adding 669 (= from Enoch's death to the Deluge according to the Hebrew Genesis), and subtracting the number in our fragment, 3,28[8 ?], from 3,237 + 669 = 3,906, the resulting date, 618 B.C., agrees perfectly with the traditional Zoroastrian date for the beginning of Vištāsp's reign (258 + 30 years before Alexander's conquest of Persia, 330 B.C.; cf. Taqizadeh, ibid., 127 sq.). From this one may infer that the famous date for Zoroaster: "258 years before Alexander" was known to Mani (Nyberg, *Rel. Alt. Iran*, 32 sqq., thinks it was invented towards the beginning of the fifth century).

<u>96</u> The name is possibly to be restored in *Türk. Man.*, iii, p. 39, No. 22, R 5, where *wy.t'δlp* was read by LeCoq.

<u>97</u> In quoting this text in *ZDMG.*, 90, p. 5, I took *wyjn* for what it seemed to be, viz. *Vēžan*. But as the appearance of *Bēžan* in connection with Vištāspa is incomprehensible, I have now restored [*'ry*]*n-wyjn*, see above, G 26.

98 For the spelling, cf. *kwdws apud* Theodore bar Kōnay.

99 *'mwst* = *amwast* = believer, faithful (not "sad" !), from *hmwd-*, Arm. *havat-*.

100 Hardly "food" or "banquet" ? Cf. Parth. *'wxrn*, etc. Also Budd. Sogd. *'wyr-* (*'wy'r-*) Impf. *w'yr-*, Inf. *'wy'wrt*, etc.) "to abandon" (*SCE.*, 562; *Dhuta*, 41; P2, 97, 219; P 7, 82; etc., appears to be of no use here.

101 Cf. NPers. *jehāniyān*.

102 Cf. *Vd.*, ii, 20 ? But the Manich. fragment appears to describe the election of Yima to the sovereignty over the world.

103 Cf. *BSOS.*, X, 102, n. 4.

104 *šyrn'm* is a *karmadhāraya*, = acclamation(s), cheering, cf. e.g. *Rustam frg.* (P 13, 5) *prw RBkw šyrn'm* "with loud cheers"; it should not be confused with the *bahuvrīhi šyrn'm'k* "well-reputed, famous" (e.g. Reichelt, ii, 68, 9; *šyrn'm'y*, ibid., 61, 2, cf. *BBB.*, 91, on *a* 11). But *šyrn'm* is also "(good) fame", see e.g. *V.J.*, 156, 168, 1139.

The Dead Sea Scroll version

A summary statement of the descent of the wicked angels, bringing both knowledge and havoc. Compare Genesis 6:1-2, 4.

1Q23 Frag. 9 + 14 + 15 2 [. . .] they knew the secrets of [. . .] 3 [. . . si]n was great in the earth [. . .] 4 [. . .] and they killed many [. .] 5 [. . . they begat] giants [. . .]

The angels exploit the fruifulness of the earth.

4Q531 Frag. 3 2 [. . . everything that the] earth produced [. . .] [. . .] the great fish [. . .] 14 [. . .] the sky with all that grew [. . .] 15 [. . . fruit of] the earth and all kinds of grain and all the trees [. . .] 16 [. . .] beasts and reptiles . . . [al]l creeping things of the earth and they observed all [. . .] |8 [. . . eve]ry harsh deed and [. . .] utterance [. . .] 19 [. . .] male and female, and among humans [. . .]

The two hundred angels choose animals on which to perform unnatural acts, including, presumably, humans.

1Q23 Frag. 1 + 6 [. . . two hundred] 2 donkeys, two hundred asses, two hundred . . . rams of the] 3 flock, two hundred goats, two hundred [. . . beast of the] 4 field from every animal, from every [bird . . .] 5 [. . .] for miscegenation [. . .]

The outcome of the demonic corruption was violence, perversion, and a brood of monstrous beings. Compare Genesis 6:4.

4Q531 Frag. 2 [. . .] they defiled [. . .] 2 [. . . they begot] giants and monsters [. . .] 3 [. . .] they begot, and, behold, all [the earth was corrupted . . .] 4 [. . .] with its blood and by the hand of [. . .] 5 [giant's] which did not suffice for them and [. . .] 6 [. . .] and they were seeking to devour many [. . .] 7 [. . .] 8 [. . .] the monsters attacked it.

4Q532 Col. 2 Frags. 1 - 6 2 [. . .] flesh [. . .] 3al [l . . .] monsters [. . .] will be [. . .] 4 [. . .] they would arise [. . .] lacking in true knowledge [. . .] because [. . .] 5 [. . .] the earth [grew corrupt . . .] mighty [. . .] 6 [. . .] they were considering [. . .] 7 [. . .] from the angels upon [. . .] 8 [. . .] in the end it will perish and die [. . .] 9 [. . .] they caused great corruption in the [earth . . .] [. . . this did not] suffice to [. . .] "they will be [. . .]

The giants begin to be troubled by a series of dreams and visions. Mahway, the titan son of the angel Barakel, reports the first of these dreams to his fellow giants. He sees a tablet being immersed in water. When it emerges, all but three names have been washed away. The dream evidently symbolizes the destruction of all but Noah and his sons by the Flood.

2Q26 [. . .] they drenched the tablet in the wa [ter . . .] 2 [. . .] the waters went up over the [tablet . . .] 3 [. . .] they lifted out the tablet from the water of [. . .]

The giant goes to the others and they discuss the dream.

4Q530 Frag.7 [. . . this vision] is for cursing and sorrow. I am the one who confessed 2 [. . .] the whole group of the castaways that I shall go to [. . .] 3 [. . . the spirits of the sl]ain complaining about their killers and crying out 4 [. . .] that we shall die together and be made an end of [. . .] much and I will be sleeping, and bread 6 [. . .] for my dwelling; the vision and also [. . .] entered into the gathering of the giants 8 [. . .]

6Q8 [. . .] Ohya and he said to Mahway [. . .] 2 [. . .] without trembling. Who showed you all this vision, [my] brother? 3 [. . .] Barakel, my father, was with me. 4 [. . .] Before Mahway had finished telling what [he had seen . . .] 5 [. . . said] to him, Now I have heard wonders! If a barren woman gives birth [. . .]

4Q530 Frag. 4 3 [There]upon Ohya said to Ha[hya . . .] 4 [. . . to be destroyed] from upon the earth and [. . .] 5 [. . . the ea]rth. When 6 [. . .] they wept before [the giants . . .]

4Q530 Frag. 7 3 [. . .] your strength [. . .] 4 [. . .] 5 Thereupon Ohya [said] to Hahya [. . .] Then he answered, It is not for 6 us, but for Azaiel, for he did [. . . the children of] angels 7 are the giants, and they would not let all their loved ones] be neglected [. . . we have] not been cast down; you have strength [. . .]

The giants realize the futility of fighting against the forces of heaven. The first speaker may be Gilgamesh.

4Q531 Frag. 1 3 [. . . I am a] giant, and by the mighty strength of my arm and my own great strength 4 [. . . any]one mortal, and I have made war against them; but I am not [. . .] able to stand against them, for my opponents 6 [. . .] reside in [Heav]en, and they dwell in the holy places. And not 7 [. . . they] are stronger than I. 8 [. . .] of the wild beast has come, and the wild man they call [me].

9 [. . .] Then Ohya said to him, I have been forced to have a dream [. . .] the sleep of my eyes [vanished], to let me see a vision. Now I know that on [. . .] 11-12 [. . .] Gilgamesh [. . .]

Ohya's dream vision is of a tree that is uprooted except for three of its roots; the vision's import is the same as that of the first dream.

6Q8 Frag. 2 1 three of its roots [. . .] [while] I was [watching,] there came [. . . they moved the roots into] 3 this garden, all of them, and not [. . .]

Ohya tries to avoid the implications of the visions. Above he stated that it referred only to the demon Azazel; here he suggests that the destruction is for the earthly rulers alone.

4Q530 Col. 2 1 concerns the death of our souls [. . .] and all his comrades, [and Oh]ya told them what Gilgamesh said to him 2 [. . .] and it was said [. . .] "concerning [. . .] the leader has cursed the potentates" 3 and the giants were glad at his words. Then he turned and left [. . .]

More dreams afflict the giants. The details of this vision are obscure, but it bodes ill for the giants. The dreamers speak first to the monsters, then to the giants.

Thereupon two of them had dreams 4 and the sleep of their eye, fled from them, and they arose and came to [. . . and told] their dreams, and said in the assembly of [their comrades] the monsters 6 [. . . In] my dream I was watching this very night 7 [and there was a garden . . .] gardeners and they were watering 8 [. . . two hundred trees and] large shoots came out of their root 9 [. . .] all the water, and the fire burned all 10 [the garden . . .] They found the giants to tell them 11 [the dream . . .]

In Enoch, The Watchers, Chapter Seven, when they made the women acquainted with the plants and cutting roots the women became pregnant.

"In the Dead Sea text entitled the Book of Giants, the Nephilim sons of the fallen angel Shemyaza, named as 'AhyÄ and 'OhyÄ, experience dream-visions in which they visit a world-garden and see 200 trees being felled by heavenly angels. Not understanding the purpose of this allegory they put the subject to the Nephilim council who appoint one of their number, Mahawai, to go on their behalf to consult Enoch, who now resides in an earthly paradise. To this end Mahawai then:

[... rose up into the air] like the whirlwinds, and flew with the help of his hands like [winged] eagle [... over] the cultivated lands and crossed Solitude, the great desert, [...]. And he caught sight of Enoch and he called to him...

Enoch explains that the 200 trees represent the 200 Watchers, while the felling of their trunks signifies their destruction in a coming conflagration and deluge. More significant, however, is the means by which Mahawai attains astral flight, for he is said to have used `his hands like (a) [winged] eagle.' Elsewhere in the same Enochian text Mahawai is said to have adopted the guise of a bird to make another long journey. On this occasion he narrowly escapes being burnt up by the sun's heat and is only saved after heeding the celestial voice of Enoch, who convinces him to turn back and not die prematurely – a story that has close parallels with Icarus's fatal flight too near the sun in Greek mythology. Resource

Someone suggests that Enoch be found to interpret the vision.

[. . . to Enoch] the noted scribe, and he will interpret for us 12 the dream. Thereupon his fellow Ohya declared and said to the giants, 13 I too had a dream this night, O giants, and, behold, the Ruler of Heaven came down to earth 14 [. . .] and such is the end of the dream. [Thereupon] all the giants [and monsters! grew afraid 15 and called Mahway. He came to them and the giants pleaded with him and sent him to Enoch 16 [the noted scribe]. They said to him, Go [. . .] to you that 17 [. . .] you have heard his voice. And he said to him, He will [. . . and] interpret the dreams [. . .] Col. 3 3 [. . .] how long the giants have to live. [. . .]

After a cosmic journey Mahway comes to Enoch and makes his request.

[. . . he mounted up in the air] 4 like strong winds, and flew with his hands like a [gles . . . he left behind] 5 the inhabited world and passed over Desolation, the great desert [. . .] 6 and Enoch saw him and hailed him, and Mahway said to him [. . .] 7 hither and thither a second time to Mahway [. . . The giants await 8 your words, and all the monsters of the earth. If [. . .] has been carried [. . .] 9 from the days of [. . .] their [. . .] and they will be added [. . .] 10 [. . .] we would know from you their meaning [. . .]

11 [. . . two hundred tr]ees that from heaven [came down . . .]

Enoch sends back a tablet with its grim message of judgment, but with hope for repentance.

4Q530 Frag. 2 The scribe [Enoch . . .] 2 [. . .] 3 a copy of the second tablet that [Epoch] se[nt . . .] 4in the very handwriting of Enoch the noted scribe [. . . In the name of God the great] 5 and holy one, to Shemihaza and all [his companions . . .] 6 let it be known to you that not [. . .] 7 and the things you have done, and that your wives [. . .] 8 they and their sons and the wives of [their sons . . .] 9 by your licentiousness on the earth, and there has been upon you [. . . and the land is crying out] 10 and complaining about you and the deeds of your children [. . .] 11 the harm that you have done to it. [. . .] 12 until Raphael arrives, behold, destruction [is coming, a great flood, and it will destroy all living things] 13 and whatever is in the deserts and the seas. And the meaning of the matter [. . .] 14 upon you for evil. But now, loosen the bonds bi[nding you to evil . . .] 15 and pray.

A fragment apparently detailing a vision that Enoch saw.

4Q531 Frag. 7 3 [. . . great fear] seized me and I fell on my face; I heard his voice [. . .] 4 [. . .] he dwelt among human beings but he did not learn from them [. . .]

Printed in Dunstable, United Kingdom